Americans at War

TIMELINE *of the*
REVOLUTIONARY WAR

Please visit our website, www.garethstevens.com. For a free color catalog of all our high-quality books, call toll free 1-800-542-2595 or fax 1-877-542-2596.

Library of Congress Cataloging-in-Publication Data
Samuels, Charlie, 1961-
Timeline of the Revolutionary War / Charlie Samuels.
    p. cm. — (Americans at war. A Gareth Stevens timeline series)
Includes index.
ISBN 978-1-4339-5916-5 (pbk.)
ISBN 978-1-4339-5917-2 (6-pack)
ISBN 978-1-4339-5914-1 (library binding)
1. United States—History—Revolution, 1775-1783—Chronology—Juvenile literature. I. Title.
E209.S26 2012
973.3—dc22

2011006536

Published in 2012 by
Gareth Stevens Publishing
111 East 14th Street, Suite 349
New York, NY 10003

© 2012 Brown Bear Books Ltd.

For Brown Bear Books Ltd:
Editorial Director: Lindsey Lowe
Managing Editor: Tim Cooke
Children's Publisher: Anne O'Daly
Art Director: Jeni Child
Designer: Karen Perry
Picture Manager: Sophie Mortimer
Production Director: Alastair Gourlay

Picture Credits:
Front Cover: Thinkstock: photos.com

Key: t = top, b = bottom
Corbis: 11, 31, 37, 44, 45t; Willam A. Bake 34; Bettmann 8t, 12t, 19, 20t, 20b, 21, 23, 25t, 25b, 28, 29t, 32t, 32b, 33, 35, 36t, 36b, 38, 40, 41b, 42, 43, 45b; Burstein Collection 6; Geoffrey Clements 10, 17; Kevin Fleming 13; Gallery Collection 9, 15, 30; Francis G. Mayer 14, 18, 22; Michael Hicholson 8b; PoodlesRock 26, 41t; **Shutterstock:** Jorge Salcedo 12b; **Thinkstock:** 5,16, 20, 24, 27, 29b, 39

All Artworks © Brown Bear Books Ltd.

Manufactured in the United States of America
1 2 3 4 5 6 7 8 9 12 11 10

CPSIA compliance information: Batch #BRS11GS: For further information contact Gareth Stevens, New York, New York at 1-800-542-2595.

Contents

Introduction

The Revolution began as a rebellion against laws and taxation imposed by the British. It ended as a determined effort to escape British rule altogether.

When the war began in 1775, many Americans did not want independence—they only wanted for the British to take their grievances seriously. They believed they should be represented in the British Parliament in London. In the face of British resistance, however, the majority of settlers in Britain's thirteen colonies became convinced that independence would be necessary.

The Course of the War

When New England militia fired on British troops at Lexington on April 19, 1775, America did not possess an army or even a single leader. Within a few years, however, it had created a force that could defeat the British army, at the time the strongest in the world. It was led by a volunteer who would become the first president of the new nation: George Washington.

To begin with, the British believed they would soon put down the rebellion. But American resistance by disorganized militia turned into American aggression by a disciplined army, which inflicted a significant defeat on the British at the Battle of Saratoga in October 1777. Another British army remained, farther south, but after more years of fighting, the Americans managed to trap and defeat it at Yorktown. Meanwhile, the colonial leaders had declared independence and announced the creation of a new nation: the United States of America.

About This Book

This book contains two types of timelines. Along the bottom of the pages is a timeline that covers the whole period. It lists key events and developments, color coded to indicate their part in the war. Each chapter also has its own timeline, which runs vertically down the sides of the pages. This timeline gives more specific details about the particular subject of the chapter.

George Washington (right, in black cloak) prepares to receive the British surrender at the Battle of Yorktown in 1781. ↓

Causes of the War

The American colonies had clashed with their British rulers for a number of years before the situation deteriorated dramatically and war became inevitable.

This picture shows British troops opening fire on a crowd during the so-called Boston Massacre in 1770. →

Timeline
1770–1772

January 28, 1770 London Lord Frederick North becomes prime minister.

April 12, 1770 London British Parliament repeals duties on paper, glass, and other commodities in the American colonies, but retains tax on tea.

1770

1771

KEY:

Politics

Northern Campaign

Southern Campaign

March 5, 1770 Boston British troops open fire on a crowd, killing five people in the "Boston Massacre."

The roots of the Revolutionary War lie in British history. In 1689, the English Parliament was given, for the first time, the right to review all new laws and taxes requested by the king. In England's American colonies, settlers believed they should have the same rights as people in England. Their colonial assemblies, however, had no right to review laws and taxes.

In the early 1700s, England, Wales, and Scotland united to form Great Britain. When Britain went to war with France, its colonies in North America fought, too. The wars were expensive, and the British needed to raise as much money as possible to pay for them.

When the wars ended in 1763, the British imposed taxes on the American colonists. Many colonists thought the new taxes unfair and avoided paying them as much as they could. There were riots against the British. On March 5, 1770, British troops opened fire on a crowd of protestors in Boston, killing five civilians.

Boston Tea Party

Tea had been popular in Europe since the 17th century and was also popular in the colonies. When the British tried to import untaxed tea from India to sell cheaply, colonists

Timeline

March 18, 1765 The British Parliament passes the Stamp Act, taxing colonists directly for the first time.

March 5, 1770 In the Boston Massacre, British troops fire a musket volley into a crowd of Bostonians, killing five people.

December 16, 1773 The Boston Tea Party. Protestors board a British tea ship and throw tea into the harbor.

March 31, 1774 Coercive Acts (Intolerable Acts) see Britain close Boston Harbor and take other repressive actions.

September 5, 1774 The Continental Congress, drawn from 12 of the colonies, meets for the first time in Philadelphia.

← The unpopular Stamp Act of March 1765 placed a direct tax on colonists for the first time.

November 1772 Massachusetts Samuel Adams forms Committees of Correspondence in Massachusetts to coordinate action against the British.

1772

November 1772 Massachusetts The Boston Assembly demands rights for the colonies and threatens to leave the empire.

George III (1738–1820)

George III became king of England in 1760. He wanted the monarch to have more personal authority over government policy. This brought him into conflict with Parliament. In 1770, George made Lord Frederick North prime minister. North shared the king's belief that Parliament should make laws for the American colonies, rather than let the colonies do it.

George III refused to ➤➤ acknowledge the complaints of the American colonists.

◀◀ This cartoon urges the colonies to unite to defeat the British.

JOIN, or DIE.

worried that it would become more difficult for colonial merchants to sell their own tea. Bostonians boarded a ship and threw 342 casks of tea into the harbor on December 16, 1773.

Intolerable Acts

This so-called Boston Tea Party led to what colonists called the Intolerable Acts. In an effort to stop dissent from spreading through New England, the British closed the port of Boston and put Massachusetts under royal government. British soldiers began seizing stores of supplies held for use by the colonial militia. These groups of citizen soldiers provided the colonies' main form of defense. Without an armed militia, the colonies would not be in a position to defend themselves against the British.

Timeline
1773–1774

1773

March 12, 1773 Virginia
Virginia establishes a Committee of Correspondence.

December 16, 1773 Massachusetts
At the Boston Tea Party, Patriots throw a cargo of tea overboard from a British ship.

KEY:

Politics

Northern Campaign

Southern Campaign

Countdown to War

By the spring of 1775, the thirteen colonies were in a state of great tension. Years of clashes between colonists and British authorities had culminated in violence at Boston. At the same time, many Americans called for a peaceful resolution to the crisis. The thought of war between Britain and its colonies was shocking to people on both sides of the Atlantic Ocean. Yet the stubborn determination of the British government to impose its will on the troublesome colonies, and the equally strong resolve in the colonies to resist this at all costs, made conflict inescapable. All that was needed was a spark to ignite it, and this soon came.

Protestors throw tea overboard at the ↧ Boston Tea Party.

Continental Congress

The Continental Congress met in the Philadelphia State House in 1774. Representatives came from twelve colonies. Congress agreed to stop buying British goods and demanded that Britain undo its new laws. Congress agreed to meet again in May 1775 to decide what action to take. By then, however, fighting had begun in Massachusetts. The Congress continued to meet until 1789 and acted as the colonies' governing body during the Revolution.

March–May 1774 Massachusetts
Britain's Coercive Acts (Intolerable Acts) against Massachusetts include the closure of the port of Boston.

September 17, 1774 Massachusetts
In the Suffolk Resolves, Committees of Correspondence decide to ignore the Coercive Acts, marking an increase in tension.

1774

September 5, 1774 Philadelphia
Delegates from all the colonies except Georgia meet at the First Continental Congress.

December 1, 1774 North America
Approved by the First Continental Congress, a boycott on British imports to the American colonies comes into effect.

Lexington and Concord

The colonists responded to the attempt to enforce the unpopular Coercive (Intolerable) Acts by attacking British troops and forcing them to retreat.

A painting depicting Paul Revere's "midnight ride" on April 18, 1775, to warn the colonists. →

Timeline
1775
January– June

March 25 Virginia Patrick Henry makes his "liberty or death" speech to the Second Virginia Convention.

April 14 Massachusetts Governor Thomas Gage is secretly ordered by the British to enforce the Coercive Acts and use force to put down "open revolution."

January

April

KEY:

- Politics
- Northern Campaign
- Southern Campaign

March 30 London The New England Restraining Act forces New England colonies to trade only with England.

April 18 Massachusetts Thomas Gage sends 700 British soldiers to Concord to destroy militia weapons stores. Paul Revere makes his midnight ride to warn colonists in Lexington.

The first shots in the Revolutionary War were fired on April 19, 1775, in a series of skirmishes known as the Battles of Lexington and Concord. Fighting broke out when the British military governor of Massachusetts, General Thomas Gage, received orders to seize the stores of arms and ammunition that Patriots, as the American colonists became known, had stockpiled at Concord, west of Boston.

A Midnight Dash

On the night of April 18, a force of some 700 British redcoats crossed Boston Harbor in boats with muffled oars. They landed at Phipps Farm, south of the road to Cambridge, and marched toward Concord. They planned to stop off at Lexington on the way to arrest two prominent Patriot leaders, Samuel Adams and John Hancock.

Despite their precautions, the British soldiers were spotted. Two messengers set out to warn Adams,

Thomas Gage was the unpopular military governor of Massachusetts.

Timeline

April 14, 1775 Governor Gage is secretly ordered to enforce the Coercive (Intolerable) Acts and suppress any rebellions, using force if necessary.

April 18, 1775 Gage orders 700 British soldiers to Concord to destroy weapons stores of the colonial militia.

April 18, 1775 Paul Revere sets off on horseback to warn the colonists of the impending British expedition.

April 19, 1775 An unordered shot starts the Revolutionary War. British troops are forced back from Lexington to Boston. Farmers and militia fire on them throughout their retreat.

April 19, 1775 Patriot siege of Boston begins.

April 21, 1775 New Hampshire militiamen march to Cambridge, Massachusetts, after hearing about Lexington and Concord.

April 19 Massachusetts The first shots are fired at Lexington and Concord. British troops retreat to Boston, where they are besieged. News of the insurrection spreads rapidly.

May 17 Canada Troops led by Benedict Arnold capture St. John's in Canada.

June 14 Philadelphia Congress establishes the Continental army, next day, George Washington is appointed commander in chief.

June

May 10 New York Forces led by Ethan Allen and Benedict Arnold capture Fort Ticonderoga, New York, which has military supplies; the Second Continental Congress meets in Philadelphia.

June 17 Massachusetts In the Battle of Bunker Hill at Boston, the British capture the hill but lose half of their men.

Paul Revere (1735–1818)

Paul Revere was a Boston silversmith and dedicated Patriot. He gathered intelligence about British soldiers, which he passed on to Patriot leaders. At around 10:00 P.M. on April 18, 1775, he rode to Lexington to warn Samuel Adams and John Hancock of the impending arrival of British troops. His ride was made famous in a poem by Henry Wadsworth Longfellow.

Patriots drive redcoats from the North Bridge in Concord. →

Paul Revere's → midnight ride is celebrated by this statue in Boston.

Hancock, and the militia guarding the arms store in Concord of the British approach. A young shoemaker, William Dawes, rode off across Boston Neck, while silversmith Paul Revere took a faster route across the water to Charlestown. By the time the British reached Lexington, around dawn, Adams and Hancock were gone. The redcoats were met on Lexington Green by 77 minutemen under the command of Captain John Parker. The British ordered the Americans to disperse. The Patriots began to give way—but then shooting broke out. No one knows who fired the "shot heard

Timeline
1775
July– December

July 3 Massachusetts George Washington takes command of the Continental army and 17,000 troops around Boston.

September 25 Canada Ethan Allen aborts his attack on Montreal and is captured by the British.

July

October

August 22 London King George III issues a proclamation declaring the American colonies to be in a state of open rebellion.

KEY:

Politics

Northern Campaign

Southern Campaign

round the world," as the contemporary Patriot author Tom Paine called it—both sides claimed that the other fired first. The redcoats then fired a volley and made a bayonet charge. The outnumbered Americans ran for cover, leaving eight dead and ten wounded. One British soldier was hurt. The British commander, horrified, ordered his men to stop firing and march on to Concord.

A Second Shot

The British arrived in Concord at 8:00 A.M. and began looking for the arms, most of which had already been spirited away. Again a single shot rang out, this time by the North Bridge. Once again, the British soldiers returned fire without waiting for orders. This time the local militia did not run; instead, they fired back. At noon, the British commander decided to retreat to Boston.

On the long march back, the weary British were repeatedly fired on by Patriots from behind walls, hedges, and boulders. During the day's fighting, the British lost 273 men and the Americans 95. The action caused a surge of military enthusiasm that led to the siege of Boston; the Revolutionary War had begun.

Minutemen

Named for their ability to be ready to fight at short notice, the minutemen came from a small elite force of special militia companies. The youngest and fittest men, they were trained to assemble at short notice to face any threat. Dating from the 17th century, about a quarter of the militia in Massachusetts were in minute companies. The minutemen were among the first Patriots to fight in the Revolution.

← This minuteman statue stands at the scene of the fighting in Concord.

November 13 Canada After an easy battle, American troops capture and occupy Montreal.

December 31 Canada Montgomery is killed during a failed American assault on Quebec.

December

November 2 Canada Under General Montgomery, Americans end siege of St. John's and take the fort.

November 28 Philadelphia Congress establishes the American navy.

Battle of Bunker Hill

Although the British won the Battle of Bunker Hill, it was a costly victory. Their casualties were high and American losses were far fewer.

This painting shows → the death of Patriot general Joseph Warren at Bunker Hill.

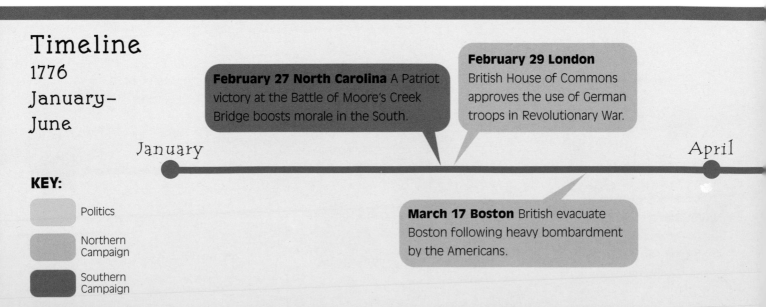

Timeline
1776 January–June

February 27 North Carolina A Patriot victory at the Battle of Moore's Creek Bridge boosts morale in the South.

February 29 London British House of Commons approves the use of German troops in Revolutionary War.

January   April

March 17 Boston British evacuate Boston following heavy bombardment by the Americans.

KEY:

Politics

Northern Campaign

Southern Campaign

British troops land in Boston in 1768 in this painting from the period.

On June 17, 1775, the bloodiest single engagement of the Revolutionary War took place on the Charlestown peninsula, across the bay from Boston.

Fighting for Position

By the middle of June 1775, 15,000 American men-at-arms had converged on Boston. More than 5,000 British troops, under the command of General Thomas Gage, were under siege in the city. When a rumor reached the Americans that Gage intended to occupy Bunker Hill, Colonel William Prescott was dispatched with 1,200 men to stop him. Prescott's forces dug themselves in on Breed's Hill, a lower height next to Bunker Hill, on the night of June 16, 1775.

Timeline

April 19, 1775 Siege of Boston begins.

May 10, 1775 Militia seize Fort Ticonderoga, near Lake Champlain in New York, with its store of artillery.

June 13, 1775 Patriots learn of General Gage's decision to occupy Dorchester Heights.

June 15, 1775 Congress votes to appoint George Washington general and commander in chief of new Continental army.

June 17, 1775 Fighting between British and American troops in the Battle of Bunker Hill sees British lose half their force.

March 4, 1776 Washington occupies Dorchester Heights and fortifies the position with artillery from Fort Ticonderoga.

March 17, 1776 The British begin an evacuation of Boston.

June 18 Canada General Sullivan evacuates his troops from Canada to Fort Ticonderoga.

June 28 South Carolina British attack on Moultrie's Fort on Sullivan's Island ends in failure with heavy losses.

June

May 2 France King Louis XVI approves sending of secret financial aid to the Patriots.

June 21 Philadelphia Thomas Jefferson shows Continental Congress his first draft of Declaration of Independence.

Henry Knox's Winter March

At Fort Ticonderoga in New York, Patriot militia seized artillery needed by the Continental army. A Boston bookseller, Henry Knox, offered to bring the guns to Boston. Knox and his men took apart the 59 guns and moved them on an arduous 300-mile (480 km) journey along rivers and across the snowy land. George Washington set up the guns in Boston in early March 1776, leaving the British no choice but to evacuate the city.

Next morning, Gage ordered warships in Boston Harbor to shell Prescott's positions. When that failed to dislodge the Americans, he sent Major General William Howe with 2,500 redcoats to secure the peninsula.

A Moral Victory

Covered by artillery fire, the British landed on the peninsula unopposed. When they charged Breed's Hill, however, the enemy was waiting. An American officer ordered, "Don't fire, boys, until you can see the whites of their eyes!" Taking heavy casualties, the redcoats retreated to regroup.

By the third British assault, the Americans' ammunition was running out, and the British finally managed to overwhelm the fortifications. The Americans retreated in an orderly fashion under cover from reinforcements brought up by General Israel Putnam of Connecticut.

The Battle of Bunker Hill may have been a victory for the British, but it was a

Knox's march is remembered as one of the great feats of the early Revolution. ⇓

Timeline
1776
July–December

July 4 Philadelphia Continental Congress approves Jefferson's Declaration of Independence.

August 27 New York A quick and comprehensive British victory occurs at the Battle of Long Island.

July

October

July 9 New York George Washington orders the Declaration of Independence to be read to the army.

September 9 Philadelphia By order of Congress, the colonies are to be known as the United States from now on.

KEY:

Politics

Northern Campaign

Southern Campaign

The fighting on Breed's Hill was recorded in this drawing of the time.

victory bought at very high cost. There were over a thousand redcoat casualties (including nearly 100 officers killed), while American losses were fewer than half that number: about 450 killed, wounded, or captured. The battle was significant because it was a clear demonstration to the British of the fighting qualities of their inexperienced opponents, whom the British had so far underestimated.

For the Americans, this first major battle against the British may have ended in defeat, but they could claim it as a moral victory. The Battle of Bunker Hill has since been honored as one of the most glorious episodes in American military history.

The Siege of Boston

Some months after the Battle of Bunker Hill, on March 4, 1776, George Washington occupied Dorchester Heights, overlooking Boston, in a single night. From the heights, Washington could bombard the British inside the city with artillery brought from Fort Ticonderoga. British officers, knowing that Boston could not be held, evacuated the city, ending the siege that had started on April 19, 1775, when the British retreated to Boston after the Battles of Lexington and Concord.

October 11–13 New York Battle of Valcour Island is one of the first fought by American navy.

November 16 New York The British capture Fort Washington and now control all of Manhattan Island.

December

October 28 New York The Battle of White Plains ends with a British victory, with losses on both sides.

December 8 Delaware Washington and his men cross the Delaware River into Pennsylvania.

December 26 Trenton Washington's surprise attack on Hessian forces at Trenton ends in victory and is a morale boost for the Americans.

Canada

The American Patriots hoped to persuade the Canadian people to join their cause against their colonial rulers. The Patriots were to be disappointed.

The Patriot general Richard Montgomery died at the start of the battle for Quebec. ⇒

Timeline
1777
January–June

January

KEY:

Politics

Northern Campaign

Southern Campaign

January 3 New Jersey Washington's timely arrival stops defeat. The Battle of Princeton ends in an American victory.

January 28 England General John Burgoyne submits a plan to isolate New England from other colonies.

April

January 6 New Jersey Washington's army encamps for the winter in Morristown.

March 8 New Jersey General William Maxwell defeats the British at Amboy.

↑ Britain's Canadian colony lay just north of the American colonies.

Timeline

1760 New France falls.

1763 Proclamation of Quebec assumes Quebec will be like other British-controlled territories.

1774 British Parliament passes the Quebec Act that allows the French majority to carry on with French laws and religion. It also expands its territorial claim into the American West.

May 10, 1775 Americans successfully attack Fort Ticonderoga.

November 13, 1775 Montreal falls to the Americans with no loss of life.

December 31, 1775 Americans fail to take Quebec. Their commander, General Richard Montgomery, is killed, and Arnold takes over.

Summer 1776 American armies withdraw from Canada.

As the Revolution began, Canadians generally rejected the arguments of the American Patriots. The Americans, meanwhile, distrusted the Canadians and their British rulers. The British had taken control of the former French colony of Quebec in 1763, and the Americans had little in common with their French-speaking neighbors. In 1774, the British passed the Quebec Act, which the Americans saw as another "Intolerable Act." The act gave freedom of worship to French Catholics. It also allowed the expansion of the province of Quebec westward—into territory that was also targeted for expansion by the thirteen colonies.

April 14 Philadelphia Congress authorizes the establishment of Springfield Arsenal at Springfield, Massachusetts. It will play a role in the Sprays' Rebellion.

June 14 Philadephia Congress adopts stars and stripes as flag with thirteen stars and thirteen stripes for the thirteen colonies.

June

April 21–28 Connecticut British destroy the town of Danbury, burning houses, barns, and storehouses.

George Washington (1732–1799)

The American commander came from a rich Virginia family. He fought in the French and Indian War (1754–1763) before joining the Patriot cause. Despite early defeats, Washington rallied his troops and turned the Continental army into a formidable fighting force. After the defeat of the British, he was elected first president of the United States.

← Patriots charge in fierce fighting around Fort Ticonderoga.

Washington came ⟩⟩ from one of the richest families in Virginia.

Heading North

After the Patriot capture of Fort Ticonderoga on Lake Champlain, New York, on May 10, 1775, the way to Canada was open. An army led by General Richard Montgomery headed north but was delayed by British resistance at the siege of St. John's. When Montgomery reached Montreal in November, the city fell without anyone firing a shot. Meanwhile, Benedict Arnold had led about 1,000 volunteers to Canada through Maine, across snowy country and along wild rivers. About a third of his force gave up and went home. Together, Montgomery and Arnold attacked the fortress of Quebec during a snowstorm on December 31, 1775. Montgomery was shot dead right at the start of the attack, which ended in a total defeat for the Americans.

Timeline
1777
July–December

July 6 New York British now occupy Fort Ticonderoga, having forced the Americans to abandon the fort.

August 4 General Horatio Gates replaces General Philip Schuyler as commander of the Northern Army.

September 11 Pennsylvania At the Battle of Brandywine, British defeat Washington and occupy Philadelphia.

July

October

KEY:

Politics

Northern Campaign

Southern Campaign

August 6 New York The Battle of Oriskany sees heavy casualties on both sides. The British move troops to leave the Patriots in control of the Mohawk Valley.

September 19 New York In the first Battle of Saratoga, the Americans block the British advance.

Canada Refuses to Join the War

The British, together with their Native American allies, had managed to keep control of Canada. George Washington sent a delegation to Montreal in 1776 to try to persuade the Canadians to join the Patriot cause, but it was unsuccessful. By the summer of that year, American armies had withdrawn completely from Montreal and Canada after a British fleet sailed up the St. Lawrence River.

The Cost of Quebec

By keeping control of Canada, the British had preserved a base from which to attack New York and New England. After a failed campaign to control the Hudson River in 1777, they used the fortress at Quebec as a base for raiding operations into northern parts of the United States until the end of the war.

Quebec's position made it relatively easy to defend. →→

Quebec

British rule was not as unpopular in Quebec as the Americans thought. The British had allowed the French way of life to continue, and the Americans were outraged that a close neighbor could be French-speaking and Catholic. Perched on a rocky outcrop, Quebec was a strong fortress city. Although Arnold's force got inside the walls, further advances failed, and British troops were able to rally.

October 7 New York At the second Battle of Saratoga, the British are forced to retreat. The American victory marks a turning point in the war.

December 18 Pennsylvania The Continental army settles into its winter camp at Valley Forge.

December

October 4 Pennsylvania The Americans fail to recapture Philadelphia in the Battle of Germantown.

Civil War

As the thirteen colonies fought numerous battles against the British through 1776 and 1777, Congress issued a Declaration of Independence from British rule.

George Washington directs Patriot troops at the Battle of Princeton. ⇒

Timeline
1778
January–
June

KEY:

Politics

Northern Campaign

Southern Campaign

February 6, 1778 France
Treaty establishes commercial relations between France and United States.

March 13, 1778 England French ambassador tells Britain that France now recognizes the United States as a country.

January

April

March 16, 1778 England Peace commission set up in the House of Commons with American Patriots.

March 20, 1778 France
Benjamin Franklin presented to Louis XVI as France officially recognizes United States.

By early summer 1776, communities in Britain's North American colonies were divided. People who supported the rebellion against Parliament were known as "Patriots" or "Whigs." But many Americans refused to challenge the king's authority. They were called "Loyalists" or "Tories."

The British Plan

King George III and his ministers hoped that British forces could encourage Loyalists to fight against the Patriots. The British plan was to send a small army from Canada down Lake Champlain toward Albany, New York, gathering Loyalist support. Then a larger force would seize New York City. That would isolate New England from the rest of the colonies. Meanwhile, another small force would occupy Charleston, South Carolina, and link up with local Loyalist forces in the southern colonies.

The plan soon went wrong. The attempt to capture Charleston failed in June 1776. The army from Canada

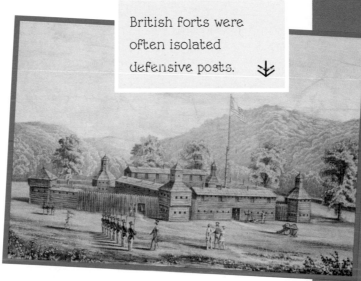

British forts were often isolated defensive posts. ⇓

Timeline

June 28, 1776 The British fail to destroy Moultrie's Fort on Sullivan's Island off Charleston.

July 4, 1776 Declaration of Independence is approved.

August 27, 1776 The loss of New York City in the Battle of Long Island marks a low point for the Patriot cause.

October 11–13, 1776 The Battle of Valcour Island sets back Britain's attempt to split the colonies; it causes a delay that leads to military disaster at Saratoga.

December 26, 1776 After Washington crosses the Delaware River and defeats a Hessian force, Patriot morale receives a huge boost.

January 3, 1777 The Battle of Princeton. Washington turns the battle in the Patriots' favor and the British withdraw.

April 22–23, 1778 England
John Paul Jones leads raids off the English coast.

June 19, 1778 Pennsylvania
Washington's army leaves Valley Forge.

June

May 20, 1778 Pennsylvania
A British victory occurs at the Battle of Barren Hill.

June 17, 1778 England
War starts between France and England.

June 28, 1778 New Jersey The Battle of Monmouth Courthouse is the last major battle of the war in the northern states and ends in a draw.

Declaration of Independence

On July 4, 1776, the Continental Congress approved the Declaration of Independence. The Declaration listed the grievances of the thirteen colonies against the British. Thomas Jefferson mainly drafted it, with help from Benjamin Franklin and John Adams. They argued the Americans had no choice but to seek complete independence.

↑ The Declaration of Independence remains a national treasure.

took too long to defeat American forces on Lake Champlain. Only the capture of New York City succeeded.

The city's fall was a huge blow to the Patriots. Morale in parts of the Continental army collapsed, and whole companies deserted. The New York area became a recruiting ground for Loyalists. Washington's remarkable recovery from the blow was early evidence that he was a remarkable leader. A victory on December 26, 1776, at Trenton, New Jersey, revived Patriot hopes.

An American artillery unit comes under fire from the British at Fort Moultrie. ⇒

Timeline
1778 July–December

July 2, 1778 Philadelphia
After British evacuate the city in June, Congress returns.

July

October

KEY:

Politics

Northern Campaign

Southern Campaign

July 5, 1778 New York Washington establishes his headquarters at West Point, a strategic point on the Hudson River.

July 29–August 31, 1778 Rhode Island
The Franco-American campaign ends in failure at the Battle of Rhode Island on August 29.

The British Advance

In 1777, British troops from New York City were due to advance up the Hudson Valley to meet the British force from Canada at Albany. Instead, the forces in New York turned south to capture the Patriot capital at Philadelphia. American forces met the army from Canada at Saratoga and forced it to surrender. The defeat ended any hope the British had of being able to isolate New England from the rest of the colonies.

☗ *Washington Crossing the Delaware* (Leutze, 1851) captured the fighting spirit of the Patriots.

Declaring Independence

Meanwhile, the Continental Congress had issued the Declaration of Independence, in which they set out their grievances against the British government. The colonists had initially set out to defend their rights as Britons. Instead, they now saw that they had to become Americans, with their own nation. They now began to seek support from other countries, particularly in Europe. The victory at Saratoga suggested that, with foreign support, their revolution might be successful.

Washington Crosses the Delaware

On Christmas Night 1776, George Washington and his men crossed the icy Delaware River. Correctly guessing the enemy would be celebrating, Washington and his men surprised the soldiers and scored an easy victory in the Battle of Trenton. This set up an easy victory against the British at Princeton, New Jersey. Trenton and Princeton ended a run of defeats that almost brought the American cause to an end and led the whole Revolution to collapse.

November 11, 1778 New York
Loyalists and Indians kill more than 40 colonials at Cherry Valley.

December 17, 1778 Illinois Country
The British recapture Fort Sackville in the Battle of Vincennes.

December

December 29, 1778 Georgia
British troops retake Savannah as the Americans are forced to retreat.

Battle of Saratoga

The American victory at Saratoga in October 1777 was the turning point in the war. The defeat of the British convinced foreign powers that the Americans might win.

General Burgoyne offers his sword in surrender to General Gates (center) at Saratoga. →

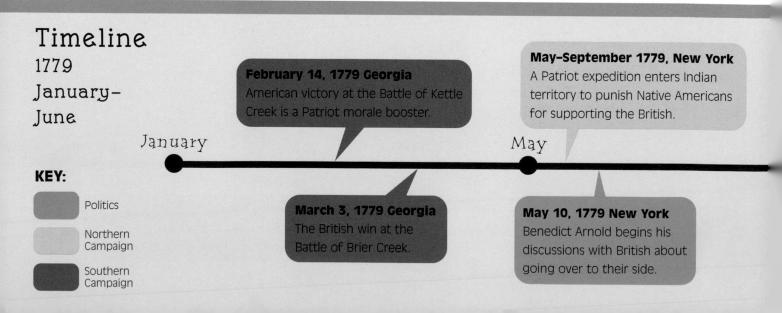

Timeline
1779 January–June

February 14, 1779 Georgia
American victory at the Battle of Kettle Creek is a Patriot morale booster.

May–September 1779, New York
A Patriot expedition enters Indian territory to punish Native Americans for supporting the British.

January   May

KEY:

Politics

Northern Campaign

Southern Campaign

March 3, 1779 Georgia
The British win at the Battle of Brier Creek.

May 10, 1779 New York
Benedict Arnold begins his discussions with British about going over to their side.

In early 1777, the British commander General John Burgoyne devised a plan to isolate New England from the rest of the colonies. Two British armies would march south from Canada, while General Howe's army in the south would march northward. All three forces would meet at Albany, New York.

Trouble Ahead

Initially, Burgoyne's army of 8,000 troops advanced steadily into New York. Heavily outnumbered, the American commander, General Philip Schuyler, decided to abandon Fort Ticonderoga and concentrate on delaying tactics. The loss of the fort led the Continental Congress to replace Schuyler with General Horatio Gates. Still, Schuyler's tactics had slowed down Burgoyne's advance and allowed time for reinforcements to arrive.

By August, the British were suffering from supply problems. In western New York, the British advance from Fort Oswego was halted by General Benedict Arnold. Burgoyne's three-pronged attack on Albany had been greatly weakened.

Timeline

Early 1777 General Burgoyne plans to isolate New England from rest of colonies.

August 1777 Supply problems hit advancing British troops.

September 13–14, 1777 Burgoyne crosses the Hudson River.

September 19, 1777 At the Battle of Freeman's Farm, an American victory is prevented by British and German discipline.

October 7, 1777 In further engagement, the British suffer losses three times as high as the Patriots; the British are forced to retreat three days later.

October 14, 1777 Burgoyne sends a letter of surrender.

October 17, 1777 Burgoyne finally surrenders at Saratoga.

← A revolutionary cannon still stands on the battlefield at Saratoga.

June 1, 1779 New York The British are able to act on Arnold's intelligence, and Clinton begins offensive up the Hudson River.

June

May 23, 1779 New York Benedict Arnold gives the British valuable intelligence.

June 20, 1779 South Carolina Battle of Stono Ferry near Charleston sees the Americans repulsed.

John Burgoyne (1722–1792)

"Gentleman Johnny" was a leader of London society. He was a member of Parliament, playwright, and soldier. When he invaded New York in 1777, Burgoyne was confident of victory, but he made a fatal error. He moved his army too far from its supply bases and advanced too slowly. That allowed the Patriots to intercept him at the decisive Battle of Saratoga.

The British Are Outnumbered

By September 1777, Patriot forces under Gates stood at 7,000 while British forces amounted to only 6,000. On September 13–14, Burgoyne crossed the Hudson River just north of Saratoga. On September 19, he engaged the Americans in battle at Freeman's Farm. The Americans outnumbered their opponents, but the superior discipline of the British and their German mercenaries (hired soldiers) was able to prevent an American victory. British losses numbered 600 casualties and prisoners, while the Americans suffered 300 casualties. Burgoyne's force retreated and fortified a position only a mile (1.6 km) from the Americans. Burgoyne learned that Sir Henry Clinton was leading 2,000 troops north to divert Gates' army. Burgoyne decided to wait for Clinton's arrival, but American raids reduced supplies and desertions increased. As the British force grew smaller, the arrival of reinforcements swelled the Patriot forces to almost 11,000.

↑ Burgoyne (in red coat) persuades Native Americans to support the British cause.

Timeline
1779
July–
December

July

October

KEY:

- Politics
- Northern Campaign
- Southern Campaign

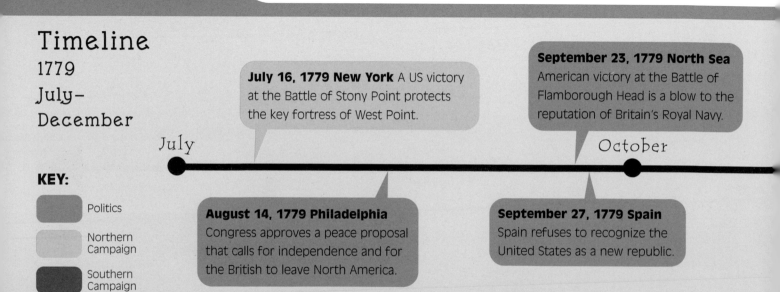

July 16, 1779 New York A US victory at the Battle of Stony Point protects the key fortress of West Point.

September 23, 1779 North Sea American victory at the Battle of Flamborough Head is a blow to the reputation of Britain's Royal Navy.

August 14, 1779 Philadelphia Congress approves a peace proposal that calls for independence and for the British to leave North America.

September 27, 1779 Spain Spain refuses to recognize the United States as a new republic.

On October 7, Burgoyne sent 1,500 troops toward the American right flank. The Americans counterattacked at Bemis Heights. British losses of nearly 600 were three times those of the Patriots.

← Washington and Von Steuben tour the camp at Valley Forge.

Defeat Beckons

With no aid from Clinton in sight, Burgoyne retreated north, reaching Saratoga on October 10. Gates's main force, now numbering 17,000, followed. Meanwhile, a 1,100-strong militia force crossed the Hudson River, cutting off any further retreat for the British.

On October 14, Burgoyne wrote to Gates asking for terms of surrender. Hopeful that Clinton might still arrive, Burgoyne delayed before finally surrendering on October 17.

← The American soldiers had to build their own winter huts at Valley Forge.

Valley Forge

In the winter of 1777, Washington's army camped at Valley Forge, Pennsylvania. The exhausted soldiers had little food or shelter and few warm clothes; nearly 2,000 died from disease. But Washington and his Prussian adviser, Baron von Steuben, drilled the troops in order to make them more disciplined. The army that left Valley Forge was a far stronger fighting force than the one that had arrived.

October 9, 1779 Georgia A Franco-American army attacks the British during the siege of Savannah; the British repulse the attack and retain control of the city.

December

December 1, 1779 New Jersey Washington establishes his winter quarters at Morristown; harsh conditions lead many of his troops to desert.

International War

In 1778, the Revolutionary War became an international conflict as France and Spain, both old enemies of Britain, joined the American cause.

HMS *Quebec* blows up ➤ during a battle with the French frigate *Surveillante* off France in October 1779.

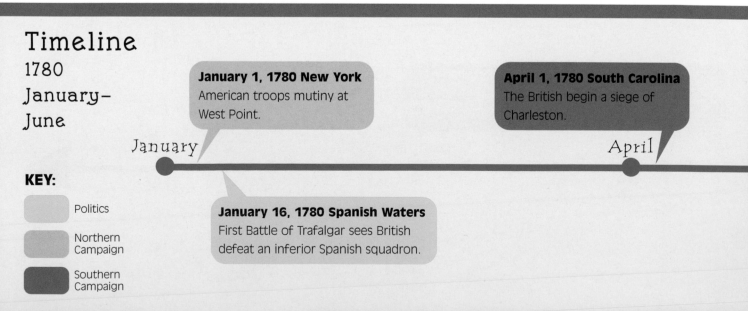

Timeline
1780 January–June

January 1, 1780 New York
American troops mutiny at West Point.

January

April 1, 1780 South Carolina
The British begin a siege of Charleston.

April

January 16, 1780 Spanish Waters
First Battle of Trafalgar sees British defeat an inferior Spanish squadron.

KEY:

- Politics
- Northern Campaign
- Southern Campaign

Both France and Spain had old rivalries with Great Britain. Both hoped that the war in North America would bring a chance to win back territory lost to the British in wars earlier in the 1700s.

France and Spain Join the Cause

America's alliance with France was the result of months of diplomacy. Benjamin Franklin had arrived in Paris, the French capital, at the end of 1776 on a mission from Congress. Franklin offered the French an opportunity to avenge its losses to the British in Canada and elsewhere in 1763, at the end of the French and Indian War. The French government gave the Americans a huge amount of cash to buy weapons and loaned them money that was vital to pay for the American cause during the winter of 1776 to 1777.

Spain was slower to join the war. The Spanish government worried that the example of the

Timeline

June 28, 1778 The Battle of Monmouth Courthouse is the last major clash in the northern states and ends as a draw.

July 16, 1779 American victory at the Battle of Stony Point.

September 23, 1779 HMS *Serapis* surrenders at the Battle of Flamborough Head.

September–October 1779 Siege of Savannah ends in British victory.

May 12, 1780 Charleston falls to the British after a siege.

August 16, 1780 General Horatio Gates flees during the Battle of Camden.

October 7, 1780 Loyalists surrender at the Battle of King's Mountain.

← *Spirit of 76*—Patriot musicians painted by Archibald Willard in 1875—is also known as *Yankee Doodle*.

May 12, 1780 South Carolina The worst American defeat of the Revolution as Charleston surrenders. British capture over 3,000 Patriots.

June

May 29, 1780 South Carolina Loyalists meet Patriots at Waxhaws in Lancaster. Patriots claim Loyalists attacked them as they tried to surrender.

Molly Pitcher

The wives of soldiers often traveled with their husbands. Some helped on the battlefield. At Monmouth, Mary Hays McCauly earned the nickname Molly Pitcher by bringing pitchers of water to the thirsty soldiers. She helped carry the wounded to safety. When her husband was injured, Molly took his place. She helped to load and fire a cannon for the rest of the battle. Molly's bravery was recognized by George Washington, who made her a noncommissioned officer.

« Washington rallies his troops at the Battle of Monmouth.

Patriots might encourage discontent in its own colonies. The Spanish did not want to encourage revolution in Mexico, Colombia, or Peru, because Spain relied on money from the colonies. However, in 1779, the Spanish began to attack British forces. They concentrated on Florida, which then reached west to the Mississippi River.

A Different Strategy

Foreign support encouraged American leaders to revise their plans. American military strategy would now focus on limiting British control to the areas immediately around the ports of New York and Newport, Rhode Island, from where they had little prospect of breaking out. At the same time, Patriot commanders sought to push American control north of the Ohio River during the Illinois Campaign.

« "Sergeant" Molly Pitcher at the Battle of Monmouth.

Timeline
1780 July–December

July

July 25, 1780 North Carolina General Horatio Gates takes command of Southern Army at Coxe's Hill.

August 16, 1780 South Carolina At the Battle of Camden, General Gates flees, ruining his reputation. British confirm their control of South Carolina.

July 30, 1780 South Carolina The capture of Thicketty Fort (Fort Anderson) precedes the Battle of King's Mountain.

KEY:

- Politics
- Northern Campaign
- Southern Campaign

The British Change Tactics

The British, in turn, decided that it was impossible to defeat the Americans in New England and the Middle Atlantic states. They withdrew their troops from Philadelphia. British leaders looked to the South. Lord George Germain, secretary of state for America, believed that Loyalists in the Carolinas and Georgia would rally to the king if a British army landed there.

In 1778, the British attacked Savannah, Georgia, starting a new phase of the war. Victories at Savannah and at the siege of Charleston would see the British eventually extend control over the South.

Jones's *Bonhomme Richard* (right) and HMS *Serapis* fire on each other. ⇣

John Paul Jones (1747–1792)

Scottish-born Jones was the Revolution's greatest naval officer and founded America's naval tradition. Jones sailed on British ships before settling in Virginia in 1773. He joined the Continental navy and, from a base in France, he raided British shipping and ports—including his former hometown. His greatest victory came in September 1779 off the east coast of England during the Battle of Flamborough Head aboard *Bonhomme Richard*.

October 7, 1780 South Carolina Battle of King's Mountain sees British invasion of North Carolina abandoned as Loyalist troops surrender.

October   December

December 21, 1780 England Britain declares war on the Netherlands after the Dutch join the League of Armed Neutrality.

End of the War

As the British found themselves fighting the French and Spanish as well as the Americans, their resources became stretched and the war moved in America's favor.

A cabin stands on the preserved site of the Cowpens battlefield. →

Timeline
1781 January–June

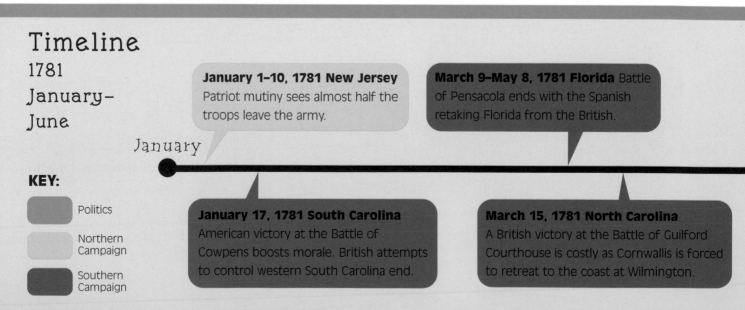

January 1–10, 1781 New Jersey Patriot mutiny sees almost half the troops leave the army.

March 9–May 8, 1781 Florida Battle of Pensacola ends with the Spanish retaking Florida from the British.

January

KEY:
- Politics
- Northern Campaign
- Southern Campaign

January 17, 1781 South Carolina American victory at the Battle of Cowpens boosts morale. British attempts to control western South Carolina end.

March 15, 1781 North Carolina A British victory at the Battle of Guilford Courthouse is costly as Cornwallis is forced to retreat to the coast at Wilmington.

↑ By 1779, the American army had developed a full range of uniforms.

With France already fighting on the American side, Spain and the Netherlands both joined the war on the American side in 1779. Both hoped that victory would bring the chance to gain foreign colonies.

The British Make Gains

In America, the British remained besieged in New York, but they fared better elsewhere. They took Charleston and narrowly failed to capture a key fort at West Point on the Hudson River. But then the one-time American hero General Benedict Arnold switched sides and tried to hand the fort to the British. In the South, Patriot

Timeline

January 17, 1781 Victory at the Battle of the Cowpens boosts Patriot morale.

March 15, 1781 The British General Lord Cornwallis is forced to retreat to the coast at Wilmington after the Battle of Guilford Courthouse.

April 25, 1781 The troops of the Prussian American General von Steuben are outnumbered and forced to retreat during the Battle of Petersburg.

March 9–May 8, 1781 At the Battle of Pensacola, Spain takes back Florida, which the British have held since the end of the French and Indian War in 1763.

September 8, 1781 At the Battle of Eutaw Springs, the Americans suffer heavy casualties before they retreat; the British, under Colonel Stewart, withdraw into Charleston, leaving South Carolina in Patriot hands.

April 25, 1781 Virginia At the Battle of Petersburg, outnumbered American militia are forced to retreat across the Appomattox River.

April

June

May 22–June 19, 1781 South Carolina The siege of Ninety-Six is an unsuccessful Patriot attack on a Loyalist stronghold.

Benedict Arnold (1741–1801)

Benedict Arnold had played a leading role for the Patriots and was considered an American hero. But in 1780, angry at not being promoted, he became a traitor. Arnold's plan to hand a key fort to the British was found out and his fellow plotter, Major John Andre, was hanged. Arnold fled to the British, whom he served as a general for the rest of the war.

Arnold's colleague Major Andre is led to execution after his trial. →

militia had more success than the regulars commanded by Horatio Gates, whom Washington replaced with Nathanael Greene in fall 1780.

Patriot Mutiny

On January 1, 1781, harsh winter conditions sparked the only major Patriot mutiny of the war. Around 1,500 soldiers from Pennsylvania insisted that their service was over. They marched to Philadelphia and asked Congress to discharge them. Two hundred were discharged while the remainder were given a furlough—or rest—and then sent back to the army.

Fortunes Begin to Change

The British troops found themselves increasingly stretched as they had to fight the French and Spanish

for control of islands in the Caribbean as well as on the American continent. They lost West Florida to the Spanish in the Battle of Pensacola, when the besieging Spanish blasted a hole in the walls of a British fort.

Timeline
1781
July–
December

July

KEY:

Politics

Northern Campaign

Southern Campaign

August 1, 1781 Virginia General Cornwallis establishes British base at Yorktown on Chesapeake Bay.

September 8, 1781 South Carolina British withdraw after the Battle of Eutaw Springs, leaving South Carolina in Patriot hands.

September 5–8, 1781 Virginia The British are forced to retreat in the Battle of Virginia Capes fought in waters off Yorktown.

September 28, 1781 Virginia Siege of Yorktown begins as Washington's army surrounds the British base.

↑ Patriots force back British redcoats at the Battle of the Cowpens.

Spain in the Revolutionary War

In 1779, Spain joined the American cause, despite worries that its colonies might want independence. Spain wanted to take back Florida, which it lost to Britain after defeat in the Seven Years' War. The Spanish gave money and supplies to the Patriots and let them use the port of New Orleans. Spanish military and naval forces were active against the British and their allies in Florida and the Southeast.

Victories on the mainland were proving costly in terms of casualties, meanwhile, so British forces planned to withdraw to coastal positions to await reinforcements. Those reinforcements were prevented by a French blockade off the Atlantic coast. The blockade also stopped supplies sent from England reaching the troops. Numerous battles fought across the Carolinas in the South eventually drove the British into a trap at Yorktown—and a defeat that would mark the end of the Revolutionary War.

« Benjamin Franklin gained French support for the American cause.

October 3, 1781 Virginia
Skirmish at Gloucester is part of the Yorktown campaign as British and French troops clash.

October 19, 1781 Virginia
Cornwallis's surrender virtually ensures American independence.

October

December

October 17, 1781 Virginia Realizing his troops are beaten, Cornwallis proposes the terms of his surrender.

Battle of Yorktown

The Battle of Yorktown was the last major battle of the Revolutionary War. With the surrender of General Lord Cornwallis, the British knew they had lost their colonies.

This engraving shows the British trapped by the Continental army on land and French ships off the coast.

Timeline
1782
January–June

February 17–June 20, 1782 Indian Ocean
The French and British clash at sea in four separate engagements.

January

March

KEY:

Politics

Northern Campaign

Southern Campaign

March 22, 1782 Kentucky
Americans fight Indians in the Battle of Little Mountain.

Although the British won almost all the battles in the Carolinas, they suffered considerable losses of men, supplies, and equipment. Their hopes of recruiting local Loyalists to swell the army's numbers failed to materialize. Few joined up, and fewer stayed for long.

After another costly victory at Guilford Courthouse on March 15, 1781, Cornwallis marched to Wilmington on the coast of North Carolina to pick up supplies and reinforcements. Next month, he took about 1,500 men north to Petersburg, Virginia, where, on May 20, they linked up with 6,000 others led by the former Patriot hero Benedict Arnold. The British then moved to the area around Portsmouth and Williamsburg in Virginia.

A Plan for Attack

Cornwallis had orders to set up a naval base for an attack on Virginia. He selected a site at Yorktown, at the southern end of Chesapeake Bay.

French ships blockaded the British position at Yorktown. ⤓

Timeline

August 30, 1781 A French fleet arrives off Yorktown to blockade Chesapeake Bay.

September 5, 1781 In the Battle of Virginia Capes, the French fleet defeats the British under Admiral Thomas Graves.

September 28–October 19, 1781 Three weeks of heavy bombardment and the capture of key forward positions sees the British forced to surrender.

October 19, 1781 Cornwallis surrenders to Washington.

October 24, 1781 Clinton's fleet arrives off Yorktown too late to help Cornwallis.

May 25–June 6, 1782 Ohio Country
Washington asks Colonel William Crawford to lead an expedition into Ohio.

June 6, 1782 Ohio Country
Crawford's supply train is attacked, and in the ensuing battle, 250 Patriots die.

May

June

June 20, 1782 Philadelphia
Congress adopts the Great Seal of the United States.

Comte de Rochambeau

Jean-Baptiste Donatien de Vimeur, count of Rochambeau, commanded the military force sent from France to cooperate with the Continental army in 1780. He had served with the French army in Europe, but had been wounded in battle. Rochambeau played a key role in the defeat of the British at Yorktown. Although he was a more experienced soldier, Rochambeau was careful to acknowledge Washington as overall commander of the allied forces.

At Yorktown, the British began building defensive works. Cornwallis knew that, while he waited for reinforcements to arrive by sea, he would have to withstand a siege from troops commanded by Washington's lieutenant, the Marquis de Lafayette.

The French Help Out

The first fleet to arrive in the area was French. Some 24 ships and 3,000 troops established a blockade across the mouth of Chesapeake Bay. This

This French map shows the position of the opposing sides at Yorktown. ⇓

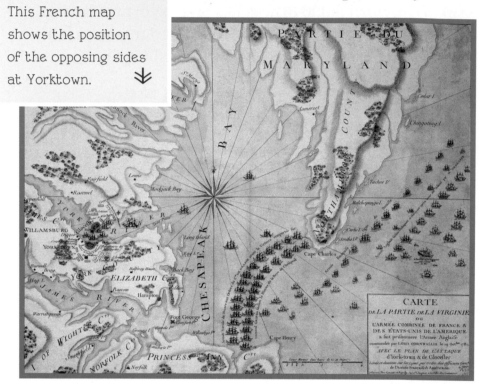

Timeline
1782
July–
December

July

September

KEY:

Politics

Northern Campaign

Southern Campaign

July 11, 1782 Georgia
British governor Sir James Wright and other British officials evacuate Savannah.

September 11–13, 1782 West Virginia
Loyalists besiege group of Americans at the Siege of Fort Henry (Wheeling).

September 3, 1782 Paris Preliminary peace negotiations, ongoing since 1780, end. Key details, including independence, still have to be resolved.

was a decisive blow: it ensured that Cornwallis' wait for reinforcements would be in vain. That gave George Washington the freedom to march 7,000 American and French troops south from New York to join the siege.

⬆ Cornwallis rides through the American lines to surrender.

The British Are Surrounded

With Washington and Lafayette blocking the way south and Rochambeau's French straddling the road west to Williamsburg, Cornwallis had no way out. His army was outnumbered, and food supplies were running low. He tried to get men across the York River to Gloucester. Some made it, but a storm scattered their boats.

Meanwhile, the arrival of British reinforcements had been delayed. It was not until October 24 that a fleet of 16 ships and 7,000 soldiers under General Henry Clinton arrived off Yorktown. By then, it was too late. On October 19, Cornwallis had surrendered his whole army to George Washington.

Peace Negotiations

In March 1782, a new government took office in London. Within a month, the first contact was made between the American diplomat Benjamin Franklin and his British counterpart, Richard Oswald. They met in Paris. In September, full negotiations began, and a treaty was agreed to in November of that year. The Americans would not approve a final treaty until the British had also come to an agreement with their French allies over territorial disputes and other claims.

October 20, 1782 Morocco The Spaniards attempt to retake Gibraltar from the British—their reason for entering the war—in the Battle of Cape Spartel.

December 14, 1782 South Carolina The evacuation of Charleston leaves no British troops in the South.

October

December

November 4, 1782 South Carolina The encounter at John's Ferry, a successful assault on a British foraging party, is one of the war's last actions.

Aftermath of the War

After the fighting finished, it took many years before America established itself as an independent nation free from the shackles of British colonial rule.

George Washington addresses the Constitutional Convention in 1787. ⇒

Timeline
1783 January– June

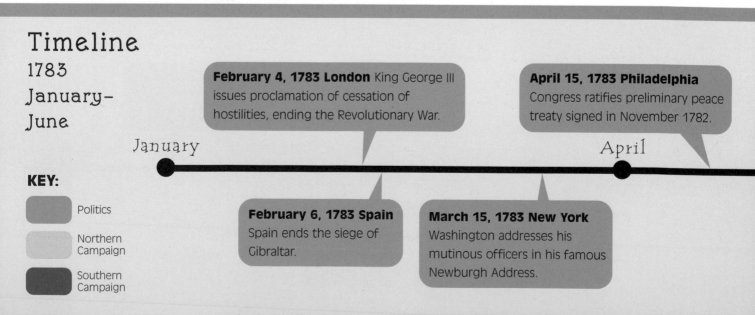

February 4, 1783 London King George III issues proclamation of cessation of hostilities, ending the Revolutionary War.

April 15, 1783 Philadelphia Congress ratifies preliminary peace treaty signed in November 1782.

January

April

KEY:

Politics

Northern Campaign

Southern Campaign

February 6, 1783 Spain Spain ends the siege of Gibraltar.

March 15, 1783 New York Washington addresses his mutinous officers in his famous Newburgh Address.

After the US Constitution had been drafted, George Washington became the first president of the United States in 1789. He served until 1797, trying to enhance unity among Americans while also creating national institutions, such as a national bank.

The United States faced many problems at the end of the war. The British still controlled important trading posts in the Great Lakes area, such as Detroit. The war had cost over $3 million, which still had to be paid. Yet there was no easy way for Congress to raise money. It could ask the states for contributions, but it could not force them to pay.

New Laws

One key success for Congress came in the Northwest Territory, which covered the area around the Great Lakes north of the Ohio River. Congress passed a law known as the Northwest Ordinance Act of 1787. It arranged for the sale of land in the region, its government as a territory of the United States, its eventual statehood, and the abolition of slavery within its boundaries. After a war against Native

⤊ The Treaty of Paris ended the Revolutionary War.

Timeline

August 1786–February 1787 Shays' Rebellion leads to changes in the new written Constitution.

May 17, 1787 At Philadelphia, delegates meet for a Constitutional Convention, which agrees a new Constitution.

July 13, 1787 The Northwest Ordinance Act allows for westward US expansion.

April 30, 1789 George Washington is inaugurated as the first president.

June 18, 1812–February 18, 1815 America and Britain fight the War of 1812.

August 24, 1814 British troops set fire to the new American capital, Washington, DC.

December 24, 1814 America and Britain sign a peace treaty in Ghent, Belgium.

April 17, 1783 Arkansas Spanish soldiers defeat British partisans at Fort Carlos.

June 8, 1783 New York Washington sends a circular letter preparing to disband his army.

June

April 19, 1783 New York Washington informs the troops of the Continental army that hostilities have ended.

June 16, 1783 Philadelphia Mutinous soldiers march on the capital demanding back pay; Congress flees to Princeton, New Jersey.

Loyalists in Canada

Many Loyalists lost their property when state governments took it to reward Patriots. Some 70,000 of the 100,000 Loyalists who left the United States settled in Canada, where the British set up the province of New Brunswick for them. Others, including Native American allies, settled in what is now Ontario. A third major area of Loyalist settlement was southern Quebec, near the American border.

Washington celebrates his inauguration as the first president in 1789. ⇒

Americans living in the area and negotiations with Britain, American control and settlement were confirmed by 1797.

The financial crisis was less easily solved. Congress could not pay the interest on its debts or pay the money owed to the people who had fought in the war. In 1786, a former army captain, Daniel Shays, led a rebellion in western Massachusetts.

A New Constitution

Shays' Rebellion, along with fears over the debt, led to the calling of a convention in Philadelphia to amend the Articles of Confederation. Instead, the convention wrote a new Constitution, which was agreed to by enough of the thirteen states in 1788 to create a new government. The bloodshed of Shays' Rebellion led the delegates to think carefully about how to

Timeline
1783
July–December

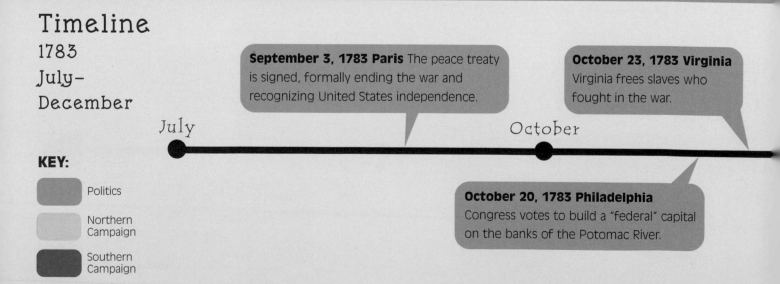

September 3, 1783 Paris The peace treaty is signed, formally ending the war and recognizing United States independence.

October 23, 1783 Virginia Virginia frees slaves who fought in the war.

July

October

KEY:

Politics

Northern Campaign

Southern Campaign

October 20, 1783 Philadelphia Congress votes to build a "federal" capital on the banks of the Potomac River.

stop the new country from falling into anarchy during times of crisis. Congress now had the right to raise taxes, the same power that had caused the British colonies to rebel in the first place.

Rebellions Continue

Washington made the war veteran Alexander Hamilton the first secretary of the treasury. Hamilton encouraged Congress to use its powers to raise money to pay the national debt. He created the first national bank and charged tariffs on imports. Hamilton also placed a tax on whiskey. It was highly unpopular. In 1794, Pennsylvania protestors rebelled against the tax. Washington led a large militia force to put down the revolt. The United States had not seen its last struggle over taxes.

Lafayette became an American hero for his role at Yorktown. »

The War of 1812

The Revolutionary War would not be the last time Britain and the United States went to war. In 1812, they fought again over the right of the British to search for smugglers on American ships on the high seas. In 1814, British troops set alight the new capital, Washington, DC. Both sides found the war expensive. With no gain to either, they signed a peace treaty at Ghent, Belgium, in December 1814.

« Citizens fight fires after a British attack on the White House in 1812.

November 25, 1783 New York The British army evacuates New York City, its last military base in the United States.

December 23, 1783 Virginia Washington resigns as commander in chief and returns to Mount Vernon.

December

November 3, 1783 New York The Continental army is disbanded at Newburgh.

December 4, 1783 New York Washington bids farewell to his officers in the Fraunces Tavern in New York City.

Glossary

artillery Cannons and other heavy gunpowder weapons.

assembly The elected representative body of one of the British colonies in North America.

blockade A barrier of naval ships that prevents other vessels sailing to or from a coast or a particular port.

colonist Someone who lives in a colony, a territory ruled by another country.

congress A formal assembly where representatives from different bodies discuss problems.

desert To abandon one's military service without permission.

dissent Disagreement with someone else's views.

flank The exposed side of a military force.

governor An official who governed an American colony on behalf of the British king.

Loyalists The name given to Americans who supported British government of North America; also known as "Tories."

mercenary A professional soldier who will fight for whoever pays him to do so.

militia A body of armed civilians who are trained to fight in times of emergency.

minutemen Elite members of the colonial militia, who were named for their ability to be ready to fight at a moment's notice.

morale The positive spirit that enables soldiers and civilians to do difficult tasks, such as fighting.

Patriots Supporters of the Americans' fight for independence; also known as "Whigs."

peninsula A thin piece of land that juts into a body of water.

redcoat A soldier in the British army, named for the color of his uniform.

siege A battle in which an enemy force surrounds a city or other position and waits until it is forced to surrender.

silversmith A craftsman who makes jewelry and other objects from silver.

traitor Someone who commits treason by betraying his or her own country.

Further Reading

Books

Battle Box: Revolutionary War. Simon and Schuster Children's Publishing, 2009.

Beller, Susan Provost. *American Voices from the Revolutionary War.* Benchmark Books, 2002.

Bobrick, Benson. *Fight for Freedom: The American Revolutionary War.* Atheneum, 2004.

Catel, Patrick. *Battles of the Revolutionary War.* Heinemann Raintree, 2010.

Deem, James M. *Primary Sources of the Revolutionary War.* Myreportlinks.com, 2006.

Earl, Sari. *George Washington: Revolutionary Leader and Founding Father.* ABDO Publishing Company, 2010.

McGowen, Tom. *The Revolutionary War and George Washington's Army in American History.* Enslow Publishers, 2004.

Micklos, John. *What Was the Revolutionary War All About?* Enslow Elementary, 2008.

Murphy, Daniel P. *The Everything American Revolution Book: From the Boston Massacre to the Campaign at Yorktown— all you need to know about the birth of our nation.* Adams Media, 2008.

Murray, Stuart. *American Revolution (Eyewitness).* DK Children, 2005.

Schomp, Virginia. *The Revolutionary War: Letters from the Battlefront.* Benchmark Books, 2003.

Websites

http://www.pbs.org/ktca/liberty/
The companion site for the PBD series *Liberty! The American Revolution.*

http://www.kidinfo.com/american_ history/american_revolution.html
Kidinfo list of links to Revolutionary War sites.

http://www.bl.uk/onlinegallery/ features/americanrevolution/ index.html
British Library site using library resources to explore the war.

http://www.historyplace.com/ unitedstates/revolution/index.html
The History Place timelines of the Revolutionary War.

http://www.shmoop.com/american- revolution/
Kids' guide to the Revolutionary War written by Harvard University postgraduate students.

Index